BRIGHT IDEA BOOKS

PINK
Dolphins

by Claire Vanden Branden

Content Consultant
Professor Tim Caro
Wildlife, Fish, & Conservation Biology
University of California, Davis

CAPSTONE PRESS
a capstone imprint

D1515580

Bright Idea Books are published by Capstone Press
1710 Roe Crest Drive, North Mankato, Minnesota 56003
www.mycapstone.com

Library of Congress Cataloging-in-Publication Data
Names: Vanden Branden, Claire, author.
Title: Pink dolphins / by Claire Vanden Branden.
Description: North Mankato, Minnesota : Capstone Press, [2020] | Series:
  Unique animal adaptations | Audience: Grade 4 to 6. | Includes index.
Identifiers: LCCN 2018058428 (print) | LCCN 2018061655 (ebook) | ISBN
  9781543571776 (ebook) | ISBN 9781543571622 (hardcover) | ISBN
  9781543575118 (paperback)
Subjects: LCSH: Boto--Juvenile literature. | Boto--Adaptation--Juvenile literature.
Classification: LCC QL737.C436 (ebook) | LCC QL737.C436 V36 2020 (print) |
  DDC 599.538--dc23
LC record available at https://lccn.loc.gov/2018058428

All internet sites appearing in back matter were available and accurate when this book was sent to press.

Editorial Credits
Editor: Marie Pearson
Designer: Becky Daum
Production Specialist: Colleen McLaren

Photo Credits
iStockphoto: aniroot, 6–7, dennisvdw, 12–13, 28, FrankMoreno, 11; Newscom: Kevin Schafer/ Minden Pictures, 16; Shutterstock Images: Christian Vinces, 19, Erica Catarina Pontes, 9, 24, 31, guentermanaus, 5, 14–15, Lisa Stelzel, 21, Mykola Gomeniuk, 22–23, Olga1955, cover, 27

Design Elements: Shutterstock Images

Printed in the United States of America.
PA70

TABLE OF CONTENTS

CHAPTER 1

PINK RIVER Dolphin

Is that a PINK dolphin? Your eyes are not playing tricks on you. The pink river dolphin really is pink!

It lives in the Amazon River. This river runs through South America. Much of the river is in Brazil. The dolphin swims in the river's dark-brown waters. It is the largest **freshwater** dolphin in the world. This animal looks like a bottlenose dolphin. But it is pink.

Some pink dolphins are part pink and part gray.

5

BLUSHING DOLPHINS

Some people think the dolphins blush when they are excited. Their cheeks turn bright pink!

Scientists are still learning about pink river dolphins. No one is sure why they are pink. Some scientists think it is because of water temperature. Others guess it is from sunlight. Dolphins in dark water can be more pink. Those in clearer water can be less pink.

A playful pink dolphin shows its belly while it swims.

The dolphin has soft, rubbery skin. It is born gray. It turns pink as it ages. Males are more pink than females.

The dolphin's body is thick. It can reach 350 pounds (160 kilograms). It grows to be about 9 feet (2.7 meters) long.

BOTO

Another name for the pink river dolphin is *boto*. *Boto* means "dolphin" in Portuguese.

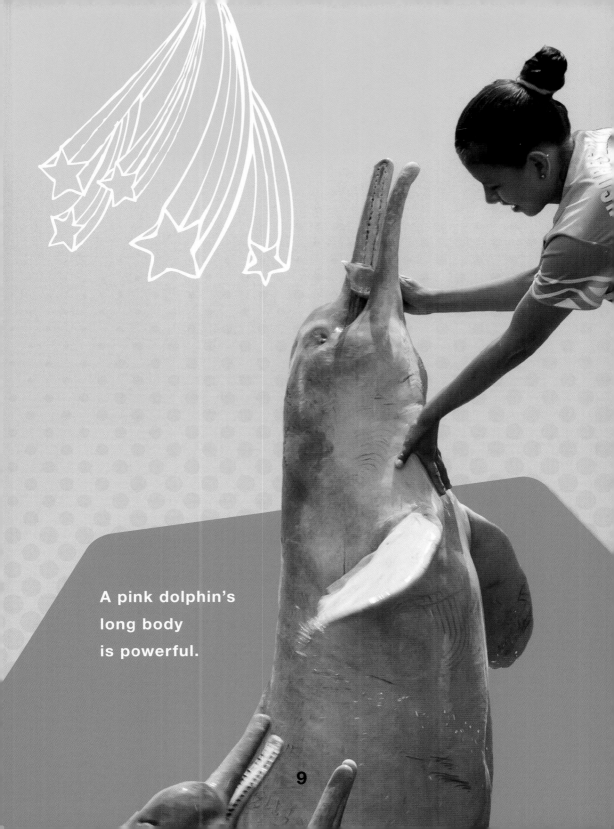

A pink dolphin's
long body
is powerful.

CHAPTER 2

SWIMMING AND Hunting

Much of the Amazon River is a flooded forest. A pink river dolphin is **adapted** to this **habitat**. Its body helps it swim around trees. Its neck bends easily. It can turn its head from side to side. Its fins can move in many directions.

One fin may move forward. The other can move backward at the same time. These traits help it make sharp turns.

Pink river dolphins can make tight turns.

HUNTING

Pink river dolphins hunt many things. They eat fish, turtles, and crabs. The dolphins have a long, skinny **snout**. It helps them snag fish on the river bottom.

NOSE HAIRS

The dolphins have tiny hairs on the end of their noses. The hairs help them sense food.

Pink dolphins hunt for food underwater.

The melon helps dolphins find food and avoid obstacles.

The Amazon River is muddy.
The dolphin's eyesight is poor.
It uses **echolocation** to find food.

It makes a clicking noise. The
clicks pass through a large **melon**.
This is a bump on top of its head.
The noise bounces off a nearby
object. Then it comes back to the
dolphin. The dolphin can find the
object from the noise.

A dolphin uses its adaptations to find and catch food.

The dolphin can change the shape of its melon. The melon can get smaller or bigger. This can change the number of clicking noises made. The melon can also change the direction of the clicks. The melon helps the dolphin find **prey** faster.

CHAPTER 3

LIFE Cycle

Some dolphins live alone. Others live in small groups. There may be two to four members.

Females give birth between May and July. They have one calf. A calf drinks its mother's milk for one year. After two or three years, a calf can live on its own. It can live for 30 years.

Dolphins traveling in pairs are often a mother and her calf.

CHAPTER 4

THREATS and Hope

It's unknown how many dolphins live in the Amazon River. But scientists say there are few left. There are many **threats** to the animals.

Humans are the biggest danger. Fishers kill the animals illegally. They use them as **bait**.

Human influences, such as plastic bottles, are harming pink dolphins.

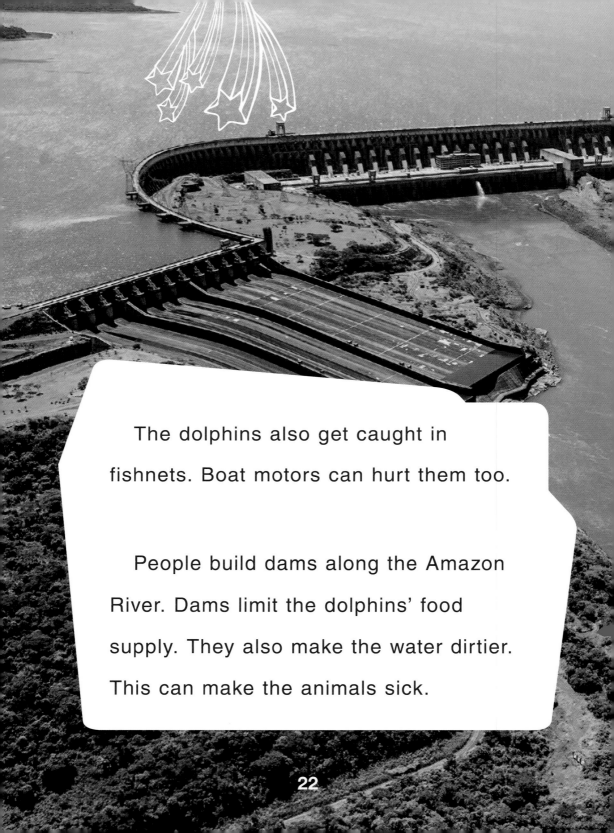

The dolphins also get caught in fishnets. Boat motors can hurt them too.

People build dams along the Amazon River. Dams limit the dolphins' food supply. They also make the water dirtier. This can make the animals sick.

Dams keep dolphins and their prey from moving from one part of the river to another.

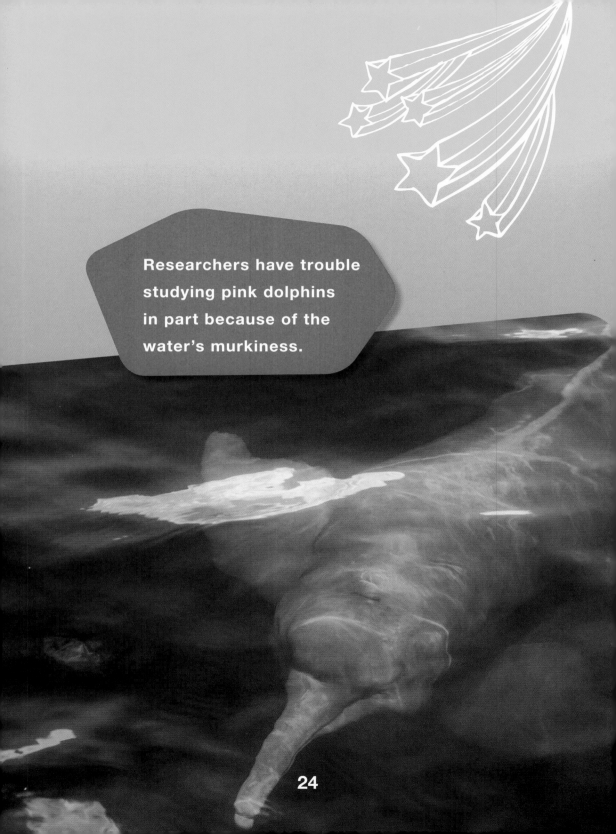

Researchers have trouble studying pink dolphins in part because of the water's murkiness.

HOPE

But there is hope for pink river dolphins. Laws help protect them. Laws limit how many fish people can catch. This way the dolphins will have enough food. But many people do not follow the laws. The dolphins are still at risk.

There are many people working to save pink river dolphins. These animals are an important part of their habitat. Many people visit the Amazon. They go there to see the amazing pink dolphins.

Many people enjoy catching a glimpse of these unique dolphins.

GLOSSARY

adapt
to have differences that help a species fit into a new or different environment

bait
something used to attract fish when fishing

echolocation
the process of using sounds and echoes to locate objects; whales and dolphins use echolocation to find food

freshwater
having to do with water that doesn't have salt in it

habitat
the place where an animal lives

melon
the round lump on top of a dolphin's head

prey
an animal that is hunted by another animal

snout
the front part of the dolphin's face that includes the nose and jaw

threat
a danger or trouble

TRIVIA

1. Pink river dolphins eat more than 50 different kinds of fish.

2. Pink river dolphins use their melons to create clicking sounds. They communicate with each other with the clicks. Together they can attack prey.

3. The Chinese white dolphin is also born gray and turns pink as it gets older.

ACTIVITY

PLAN A PINK DOLPHIN SIGHTSEEING TRIP!

You've learned about pink dolphins. Now it's time plan a trip as if you could see one in person! To do that, you'll need to plan a pretend vacation to South America. But how will you get there? And where will you stay? How will you find the pink dolphin?

First, make a budget for your trip. Then research areas where the dolphin has been seen. Don't forget to research what kind of clothing you'll need and what time of year is best for visiting South America. Write everything in a notebook. Then present your trip to your class. Be sure to include fun and exciting photographs of what you'll see on your trip!

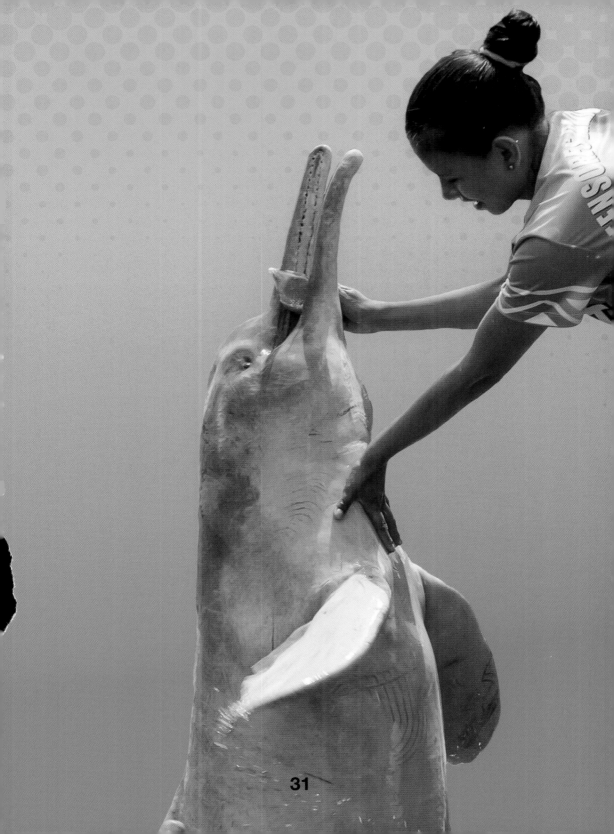

FURTHER RESOURCES

Interested in dolphins? Check out these resources:

Animal Planet Chapter Books: Dolphins! New York: Time Inc. Books, 2018.

Furstinger, Nancy. *How Do Dolphins Sleep?* Crazy Animal Facts. North Mankato, Minn.: Capstone Press, 2019.

National Geographic Kids: Pink River Dolphins
https://kids.nationalgeographic.com/videos?videoGuid=285a9018-aa5a-4d73-a3b9-e0b552090466

Want to learn about other animal adaptations? Read more with these books:

Rajczak, Kristen. *20 Fun Facts About Mammal Adaptations.* Fun Fact File. Animals Adaptations. New York: Gareth Stevens Publishing, 2017.

Taylor, Barbara. *Stinky Skunks and Other Animal Adaptations.* Disgusting & Dreadful Science. New York: Crabtree Publishing Company, 2014.

INDEX